GODDESSES

The ones who made us, the ones who healed us, the ones who saved us.

GABRIELLE G.

Cover by Gabrielle G.
All Illustrations by Zab C.
Poems and Formatting by Gabrielle G.

First Printing, 2022
ISBN :978-1-7774882-4-6

Gabrielle G.
PO 40527
Kirkland, QC
H9H 5G8 CANADA
www.authorgabrielleg.com

"The Goddess doesn't enter us from outside; she emerges from deep within. She is not held back by what happened in the past. She is conceived in consciousness, born in love, and nurtured by higher thinking. She is integrity and value, created and sustained by the hard work of personal growth and the discipline of a life lived actively in hope."

Marianne Williamson

FINDING GODS

I threw my anchor into a deeper truth
And discovered the secrets of love, heroism, and youth,
So I dove within and looked beyond eternity
And prayed the Goddesses for the gift of poetry.

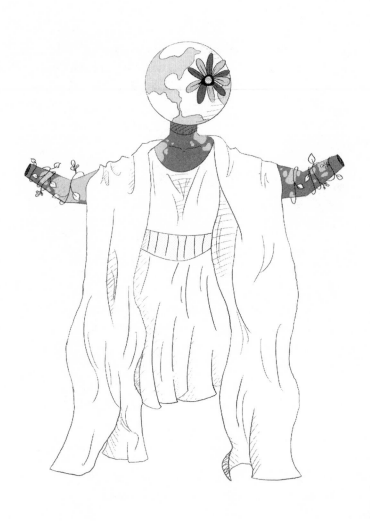

GAIA

FIRST DEITY THAT CAME OUT OF CHAOS IN THE BEGINNING OF TIME. SHE IS THE PERSONIFICATION OF EARTH AND THE MOTHER OF ALL LIVING THINGS.

AS THE MAINSTAY OF HUMAN CIVILIZATION AND PROSPERITY, ALL OR MOST GODDESSES ARE REFRACTIONS OF HER IN HER OMNIPOTENCE; SHE WAS THE FIRST, AND THOSE WHO CAME AFTER, EACH HAD A PORTION OF HER POWERS.

SHE IS THE MOTHER OF THE HEAVENS WHO PROTECT HER, AND THE MOUNTAINS AND THE SEA WHO SHAPE HER.

MOTHER OF CYCLOPES, TITANS AND HECATONCHEIRES, SHE BECAME IN TERRIBLE PAIN WHEN URANUS (THEIR FATHER) FORCED THE LAST SET OF MONSTERS BACK INTO HER BECAUSE THEY HATED HIM. SHE ASKED THE HELP OF THE TITANS FOR REVENGE BUT ONLY CRONUS ANSWERED. FROM URANUS' CASTRATION, THE BLOOD GAVE BIRTH TO THE SPIRIT OF VENGEANCES, THE GIANTS AND SOME NYMPHS. FROM THE FOAM WAS BORN APHRODITE.

THE BIRTH

And from my blood grew flowers,
From my tears bloomed springs,
Mountains formed under my powers,
And birds flew from my wings.

Ocean expanded from my heart,
Wilderness spread from my shivers,
And from my desire came art,
While my veins traced rivers.

But from my fate came the pain,
Of all mothers for their children,
And with it came the rain,
And the secrets we keep hidden.

LEGEND, TALES AND OTHER MYTHS

Religious upheaval
World uncertainty
Frightening changes
Withered society
Times of fears
Comforted in stories
New frontiers
Shared in history
Future vision
Linger in memory
Tales tensions
Known for centuries
Jumbled contradictions
In the legends we believe
Bring us to reasons
And test our values to grieve.

FORGIVENESS

Risen from Chaos to be Everlast,
We take what we want and don't learn from our past.
Celebrating you for a day of repentance,
We forget our duties and await your vengeance.
But as no one ever heard of the myth of Uranus
Who you created to protect yourself from us?
He took what he wanted and caused you terrible pain,
And then was punished with passion and blood rain.
Even if from this violence is born Aphrodite,
We shouldn't disrespect
Who holds the fate
Of humanity.

THE FOUR ELEMENTS

I drink from the rivers and the springs of sorrow,
Parched on the lies of your no tomorrow…
I feast on mountains, and skies and clouds.
Away from my pride and its lightning shroud…
I breathe in the wind of despair and heartaches,
Exhaling all my doubts and their crawling snakes…
I blaze on my guilt and scorch on my pain,
Vulcanizing my life and slowly turning insane…

CARRY ON

Inside of me
Is the strength of women
Inside of me
Are the words of their shame
Inside of me
Is the fire they ignite
For every three
I fought like a knight
Inside of me
Is the stake of witches
Screaming to thee
To welcome anarchies
Inside of me
Is the power of love
The guarantee
I'll survive all men's gloves
Inside of me
Are all my ancestors
Ready to spree
On all my oppressors
Inside of me
Is the strength of women
Wanting to free me
From all of my shame

MOTHER KNOWS BEST

It wasn't the dirt under my nails,
That gave my crime away…
But the blood left of the trail
By the tears of my prey.
"Dirt cleans easier than blood"
My mother used to say…
If only I had listened,
Instead of playing the day…

LIFE

Tethered to a hospital's bed,
Brought down by drugs,
My life looks like skittles
Swimming in my blood.

I live without living,
Out of my mind,
In a mental prison,
Time not so kind

Laughing at my symptoms,
Vitreous humour…
I survive as victim,
Of my sense of tumor.

Headache after heartache,
My body gives up.
It's another earthquake,
Filling my death cup.

WOMANHOOD

We take care of our own,
Through depression and broken bones,
We never leave a friend in need,
Alone during a mental stampede.

We never turn our backs,
To the heartbroken under attack,
From their past or love missiles,
Don't run away, blow the whistles.

We support one another,
From sisterhood and earth mother,
Because women aren't witches,
Throwing others into ditches...

We hold onto each other tight,
Through life and all its frights,
We stand strong shoulder to shoulder,
And scream our names to be bolder .

We take care of our own,
But selfishness is what you've shown,
Nonetheless I forgive you,
Because I'm not someone like you.

MY STORY

I gave you my heart, mind and soul,
Only for you to force me watch it burn…
But, pinned against a wall, sweating from fear,
I resurrect from my pain with the illusion of your
    snare.

MOTHER EARTH

I am all light and power,
I am all of the mothers
From my womb came your nature,
And from my heart rose nurture.
I am equal love and eros,
Wars, wisdom, and pathos
Mountains, oceans and skies,
Underworld and tortured lies.
I am the air you ghastly breathe,
And the life you foolishly seize,
You owe me worship and respect,
But like all mothers, me you neglect.
You destroy me one tree at a time,
And blame me for all your crimes,
But when I implode what will you do?
Will you kill Luna and Mars too?

HERA

Goddess of marriage, worshipped as queen of heaven. one of the twelve Olympians and the sister and wife of Zeus. Hera rules over Mount Olympus as queen of the gods.

Best known for her jealousy because of zeus numerous affairs with goddesses, nymphs or humans, the many myths related to her describe her persecution of zeus' lovers.

Not only know to be revengeful, Hera exhibited devotion to her favourites who were rewarded with success and love.

ZEUS IS AN ASSHOLE

The drips of your sorrow soaked my eye sockets,
With words like "Tomorrow" crumbled in your pocket.
The heart you gave others sticks to my flat chest,
Honey that flies fathered with shit on their fuck-breast…
I stitch the betrayal of my own salvation,
Knowing being loyal is just a perception…
But as I wash my sins on our promise of lies,
I pasture my foreskin and suddenly apprise.

EQUAL

It is not because I am a wife
That I am weak.
It is not because I am a daughter
That I can't speak.
It is not because I am a woman
That I can't pique.

I was born from the same God
Who has given you powers,
So don't think of me only as smiles and flowers,
Because if society has made me a fraud
I am in fact a havoc born to wreak.

SUSPICIOUS

I will burn every one of your lovers,
Destroy their hopes and druthers,
If I discover you betrayed me
And entertain their envy.

I will set fire to your mind,
With desire and wine,
If I learn you shared yourself
Without being forced or withheld.

I will ignite sweet vengeance,
With no regret or repentance,
If I discover you lied
And did more than just eyed.

I will reduce you to ashes,
With broken heart and knife's gashes,
If I learn your love was fake
And you seduced me to ease your ache.

I will then blaze my own life,
Without a word left or any strife,
As I won't bear the crushing weight
Of breathing without my soulmate.

PERVERTED

Double heart clicks on the tits of love,
Black skulls burning the passion you erode,
If some write poetry with the tip of their nipples,
Others wet their panties with words they can't decode.
And while silence takes over the real conversations,
You give all your answers with arguable actions.
And while I suck on the lollipop of regrets,
You make sure to show me, I'm the one you'll forget...

FOG AND THUNDER

I'm numb but tears drown my thoughts.
I'm tired but prayers are never sought.
I'm worried but still carry our cross.
I'm in agony but chill over your loss.
There are no words and not much time.
No magic world where our pains don't rhyme.
I love you through deep scars and blood.
Please don't corkscrew your hell in clouds.

CANNIBAL

I have sipped your lies,
And devoured your eyes,
But as I bring your heart to my lips,
I feel my soul eclipse.

MATERNAL PAIN

Worms growing inside of me,
Fearing how dark your thoughts might be,
Heart broken by your distress,
I call upon the universe…
Love dimming in your blue eyes,
Your arm covered with butterflies,
Hidden under, the deepest scars,
I pray to see some shooting stars…
Asking the sun to brighten your smile,
And the moon to protect my child,
My voice bounces like an echo…
With no effect on tomorrow.
I see the gush and clean the blood,
Swim across the guilted mud,
Weak on my knees, I am useless…
Against yourself, I'm powerless.
Worms growing inside of me,
Hurting yourself makes you feel free,
But when the blade slashes your skin…
It is my blood that drips chagrin.

BLEEDING SOUL

Please don't slash the skin,
I have given you.
Don't use the blade of sin,
On the arms I made you...
Don't let your darkest thoughts,
Guide your existential pain.
Don't believe the knots,
Your mind has chained.
Don't harm your young self,
To release your anger.
Don't feel so compelled,
To hurt for answers.
Let me clean the blood stains,
And mend to your scars.
Let me help you drain,
The tears of our stars.

MARRIAGE PLEA

Take me home,
Where I feel safe
Where love blooms
And no guilt chafes.

Take me home,
Where I belong
With no promise
Or lying song.

Take me home,
Tight in your arms
Hug my sorrow
Quiet my storm.

Take me home,
Carry my pain
Open your heart
Help me be sane.

Take me home,
Simply love me
Others haven't
And destroyed me.

Take me home,
Please hear my plea
I was a whore
Please forgive me.

27 YEARS AND COUNTING

I have carved on my skin,
hearts that beg for love,
words that blossom hate
and birds flying backwards.

I have inked in my veins,
songs that bleed my pain,
memories that never dance
and smiles depicting sadness.

I have hewn in my soul,
touches that sore my tears,
looks that soothe my wombs
and fires craving my demons.

I have bruised in my heart,
kisses that scream my fears,
thoughts that open my wounds
and impulses to have you near.

But mostly I've prayed daily
For the warmth of your laugh,
The peace of your presence
and the advice of your ghost.

POWERLESS

I want to share the light I see in your heart,
Receive the kindness you see as a weakness,
I want to be stronger to help you walk your path,
Open all minds and souls to your uniqueness.
I want to protect you from every attack,
Carry the fear I see in your stubbornness,
I want to admit I don't have any of the answers,
And become a novice in the judgements that govern us.
I want to dry your tears and promise a bright future,
Not having to deceive when I tell you to trust,
I want to embrace the pure and fight everything for you,
Because you deserve more than always being shushed,
I want to give you everything a mother can do
But all I can do right now is simply loving you.

THE PEACOCK

Resurrection and paradise,
Bird with a thousand eyes,
Gentle giant of my bleeding heart,
Your smile is what ended me hurt.

Power and royalty,
Throne bejeweled by jealousy,
Shining colours tempting my luck,
Beloved beauty having me struck.

Prayers and seduction,
Illness, old age, death's salvation,
The devils entered my soul's kingdom,
And stole the voice of your wisdom.

Fallen from grace and all blessings,
Pretentious feathers hiding feelings,
Gods' judgments await your fate,
While you parade in your mistakes.

HECATE

GODDESS ASSOCIATED WITH THE UNDERWORLD, NIGHT, AND WITCHCRAFT. SHE WAS GIVEN HER WIDE-RANGING AUTHORITY ON EARTH AND SEA AS WELL AS IN THE HEAVENS BY ZEUS.

KNOWN FOR HER CRITICAL ROLE IN THE EXPEDITION OF JASON THROUGH MEDEA, SHE IS ALSO A WITNESS IN THE ABDUCTION OF PERSEPHONE BY HADES, BUT STAYED LOYAL TO ZEUS WHO HONORED HER ALL ABOVE OTHERS.

EKATA

Over Heavens, Earth and Seas
I hold my flaming torch,
Helping those who seek
Loved ones in night's gorge.
I stand at the crossroads
Of life, fate and death,
Working from afar,
For witches' last breaths.
Ruler of darkness
I am as good as evil,
Barking hound for witness
I worship all upheaval

WORSHIP

When my heart and mind erupt a fight
And my soul screams in the night
I turn toward necromancy,
Spirits, witchcraft, and alchemy.
But when even those fail,
I turn toward old myths and tales
And slowly soothe my misery
By living amongst Gods' cruelty…
Revenge, sacrifice and punishment,
Escort me in wonderment,
And with fantasy for shadow,
I soothe my pain and my sorrow.

MYSTICAL

I wish silver would burn my skin
Or wood would poison my heart,
As I am the monster of all your sins
Deserving death for the ones we hurt.

THE TOURIST

I vacationed in Hell
And came back a survivor,
Tourist under the spell
Of being a writer.

Through pain and all the tears,
I fell on my knees.
In words, disappeared,
Befriended a sleaze.

Releasing my demons,
I lost myself to flames.
Listened to their scheming
And let them take their claims.

I became ashes
Of whom I used to be,
And lost my chances
To be loved wholeheartedly.

So, I burnt my own heart,
Screamed out years of pain,
Lost my voice and exerted
Myself from my past chains.

Gushing are still the wounds,
But my mental is strong…
Despite Satan's hounds,
I rebirth from a song

GABRIELLE G.

I vacationed in Hell
And came back a survivor,
Breaking all the spells
Of my mind's tormentor.

TRANSFORMATION

Walking through the mist, I find my path
To what I've dismissed, because of wrath.

I answer the call, nature has made,
Forgetting the sprawl, cities have laid.

I hear the whispers, of my ancestors;
The witches and sisters, dead under pressure.

They tell me all stories, share their magic spells,
Their deaths like quarries, rotting in dark cells.

I listen and learn, from the voice of wisdom,
They ended up burned, but were no victim.

As the morning brume lifts, I slowly discover,
I carry the gifts, of their occult power.

I feel it in my heart, it boils in my veins,
It's roaring for a start, something I can't contain.

Filled with enchantment, I leave the forest,
With the new contentment, that I am a sorceress.

THE HEALER

With stardust in my veins
Calming my fluttering nerves,
And rainbows in my brains
Holding all my life's curves,
I concoct word potion
For the lonely, broken souls
Who have known dejections
And fell out of control.
I breath all of their pain,
Take refuge in incantations,
Swallow their golden chains,
And save them from damnation.
With fire in their soles,
They take off like small birds
Weightless and whole
And out of this world.
I exhale their magic,
Cry the traumas of rain,
Ground myself in tragic,
And celebrate with champagne.
Tomorrow others will come
Broken, sad and full of itch...
My journey has only begun
I'm the pathetic's witch.

WITCH HUNT

Moral Panic
Barbarian acts
Love's tragic
Wizardly pacts
Widespread famine
Ruined heart
Rotten Jasmine
Edible dirt
Inhuman storms
Sadden fortune
Saboteurs' forms
Fated future
Unearthly guests
Treacherous skies
Dismissive quests
Malicious rise
Ancient power
Brand new fear
Prankster richer
Brain cells smeared

CONCEDE

I lean into destiny
And its flame of serenity,
Find my peace in giving
A part of me that was aching.

I lean into the magic,
Of the universe and its tricks,
To help sooth my sorrow
And breathe into my tomorrow.

I lean into the faith,
I have in the beyond…
In love and calmness, I bathe,
In fate's arms, I belong.

WOMANIZER

I walked across a thousand skies
To find a man for whom I'd die,
But never thought he'd be the one
Holding my life at gun's point.

I swam through oceans of pain,
Blood dripping from fate disdain,
And froze ashore the cruelty
Of every creature of the dark sea.

I slept for hundreds of years,
Shredded by sharp icebergs' tears,
And felt my soul liquified
Under the heat of lies and pride.

I woke under a stormy night,
Emptied of pain, too weak to fight…
But still rose with all my thorns,
Reborn demons without horns.

And so I fed on honesty,
Growing stronger in all beauty,
Believing love was a treason…
Spoiling my blood like a poison.

But then walking through mystic skies,
I found a love ready to die…
So, I did what everyone'd have done,
I aimed at his heart and shot my gun.

WOMEN'S VOICE

Should women always be punished
For carrying wombs that create and nourish,
The human despair of reproduction
And the men's ego of retaliation?

Robbed of their chance to be a mother
Or forced to be one by strength and power,
Used like vessels or genetic pools,
With no one to talk to and everyone screaming fool.

Should they protect their child and live under terror
Or starve their family to protect their honour?
What would you do if in danger was your life?
What would they do if those women were their wives?

Pride and injustice are how men rule,
With women's hymens treated as precious jewels
But for those monsters there is no redemption,
No God will forgive women's annihilation.

MAGICAL ADVICE

I've had to let go
A lot of my past,
So that tomorrow
Could heal and last.

I've had to mend to
Unresolved trauma,
Make for myself new
Memories from coma.

I've had to put words
On my soul's bruises,
On dead childhood birds,
And all my losses.

I had to cry alone,
Rock myself to sleep,
While I was thrown stones,
Discarded like a creep.

I was made stronger,
By my friends' abandon…
And my heart got sweeter,
With my own compassion.

Please never give up,
On curing all wounds.
Never drink the death cup,
Offered by the hounds.

GHOSTED

I am not a poet,
Neither of any God,
I write my "feelings"
And my words are sharp-clawed.
You might not understand
Every rhyme that you read,
Or like my poems,
Nonetheless, I will bleed
White hearts for nobodies,
Through tears, sweat and pain,
The art of faking,
Dancing lies in the rain…
'Cos you mean nothing more
Than actions I display,
Social media whore
I am what I betray.

DEMETER & PERSEPHONE

DEMETER: GODDESS OF AGRICULTURE WHO LOST HER
DAUGHTER TO HADES (HER BROTHER) AFTER BEING
BETRAYED BY ZEUS, SHE LOOKED FOR HER WITH
FEROCITY.

PERSEPHONE: DAUGHTER OF DEMETER. SHE BECAME THE
QUEEN OF THE UNDERWORLD AFTER HER ABDUCTION
BY HADES, THE GOD OF THE UNDERWORLD. THE MYTH OF
HER ABDUCTION, HER SOJOURN IN THE UNDERWORLD AND
HER TEMPORARY RETURN TO THE SURFACE REPRESENTS
HER FUNCTIONS AS THE EMBODIMENT OF SPRING AND
PERSONIFICATION OF VEGETATION.

PERCEPTIVE

Flowers at my feet,
Stems in my hand,
Spring cannot beat,
The discord of my land.

Through storms and fight,
Rain and thunder,
The endless white,
Darkened my wonders.

It melts all hopes,
Brews all emotions,
And suddenly elopes,
With summer's passion.

But soon it will come back,
Once the harvest is done,
And the frost will whack,
The colours of autumn.

KIDNAPPED

Be thankful for what's on your table,
As it took the heart and flesh of a Goddess
For us to feed our souls…

DECEIVED

Wouldn't you have wanted
To see the world expire
If your flesh had been stolen
Forced to love your brother.
And if your family,
Would've taken his side
When you never did
Anything improper,
But to make the Earth bloom
So, humanity doesn't know hunger?

What if the love story so many love to retell
Was only a conspiracy from oppressors
Who never knew boundaries?

A tale of the worst bullies
Sacrificing someone's daughter
For a man to queen his jail?

Is her story still romantic,
When we project our own blood
Or are you being frantic
Cleaning your soul from rape's bud?

UNDERWORLD

The pain didn't only shatter my heart,
It burnt my mind,
Woke my darkest thoughts,
And punctured my soul.
In this story, the knight saved himself…
While the princess lived in Hell.

YOU

Guilt is the slowest poison,
That can flow in our veins.
But it's also a secure prison
Where demons take their claim.

DISGUISED

I wander the Earth,
Under the cloak of Demeter,
Burning sage and myrrh,
For deception to be sweeter…
But it's in my vengeful heart
That I find the strength of life
I will drag traitors in dirt,
For ignoring my child's strife…

SPRING

"I am death"
I was expecting you
"I am death"
I am ready to outlive you
"I am death"
the stars said I can fight you
"I am death"
Nonetheless I won't kill you
"I am death"
Instead, I'll rescue you
"I am death"
And light will bath you
"I am death"
Until winter passes through
"I am death"
I will learn to love you
"I am death"
And while our passions skew
"I am death"
Life will come and bloom new
"I am death"
As I am your dream come true.

PERSEPHONE

I spend my life listening to dead people.
I like the sound of their unbreathing,
The mute whispers of their voices in the night…
And the unbeating thump of their hearts.

HADES

He was fresh hell and clear water,
Tears of the heart and dead whisper,
Poisonous eyes on blooming scars…
Criminal mind of shouting stars.

He smelled of love and old bookshop,
And found his youth in fire drops,
But if his smile subdued and harmed,
His best weapon was in his charm.

He ruled over revenge and sins,
His breath was inked on human skins,
His looks were lust on waffle cones…
And bruised your soul with winks alone.

And all his words were moans and sighs,
With pride, he watched his sinners die,
Torturing them with all their fears…
He never stopped until blood smeared.

QUEENED

Tears of guilt water my sinking heart
Letting it bloom from a dying hope,
Praying Gods' rescue while I fall apart
In the arms of those holding my ropes.
Masked puppeteer under truthful lights,
Smiling for stealing the souls of sinners,
Rightful pretentious with spade of spite,
And friendships tarnishing everyone's mirrors.
The knife of betrothal pressing on my throat,
While the spoon of love enucleates my eyes,
Blind, naked and mute, I dissolve their gloat,
So from the edge of life, perfectly healed, I rise.

ATHENA

GODDESS ASSOCIATED WITH WISDOM, HANDICRAFT, AND WARFARE. SHE IS THE PATRON OF DEFENSIVE AND NECESSARY WARS . BORN FROM THE SKULL OF ZEUS, SHE STAYS UNMARRIED AND VIRGIN BUT WAS THE ADOPTIVE MOTHER OF THE CHILD BORN FROM THE SEMEN SPILLED ON EARTH WHEN HEPHAESTUS ATTEMPTED TO RAPE HER.

KNOWN FOR HER ANGER, IT WAS ALWAYS DIRECTED TOWARD ARROGANT MEN WHO TRIED TO CHALLENGE HER BUT NEVER REALLY COULD BEAT HER WISDOM.

REQUITE

You made me nothing more than tears of dust,
From the hammer of Thor, twirling in wind's lust

Landing on new ground, I disappear on Earth,
Fragile and unowned, through blood and death…

I let my roots grow, strengthening my hold.
Despite cold and snow, I slowly unfold.

I blossom under rays, of love and compassion,
Forgetting the disarray of my past assassin.

And once tall and powerful, with only light for armor,
To you I come all revengeful and kill you with ardor.

SLITHERING SPASMS

Slowly seducing the snake of your sins,
I succumb to its song and the swell of its skin…
Your smile saddles my strength and strangles my sanity,
Suddenly I surrender and sink in sensuality.

NO HOPE FOR HUMANITY

Spreading hate not love
Is now what we're used to
And when children ask for truth
We treat them like pariah too.
Focusing on our pandemic navels
We never look further than our masks
And while some enjoy their rights enabled
Others obey and do what was asked.
But always thinking what's best for them
Always pondering what others will do next
Because our thoughts have become brain phlegm
Because hate is always our disguised pretext.

SHREWDNESS

Through millennia and centuries,
We fought for land and wealth,
For love, revenge, and misery
For oppression, freedom, and health.
But have we ever fought
In the name of wisdom?
Or are all wars just jokes?
Spells from gods' kingdoms?

HEPHAESTUS

I found solace in your pain,
Knowing you bled the loss of me,
And from your tears bloomed restraint
In the Goddess I was meant to be.
With my armor of betrayal,
I protected my nursery,
And with your truth on denial.
I carried through adversity.
Born from the heart of wisdom,
And the brain of your enemy,
I'll find revenge on your kingdom,
By starting wars infectiously.
You died alone, killed by men,
That erased you from memories
A small penalty for raping a virgin,
A price to pay for thumping history.

DISSOCIATION

I'm not here
So I don't feel his mouth right against my neck
I don't feel how his tongue's making it wet
I'm not here
And neither are his hands around my wrists
Holding me tight while stealing a forbidden kiss
I'm not here
As my legs force open for what must come
I don't feel his weight while dryness hurt and burn
I'm not here
And neither are his flesh, lust, or putrid skin
My eyes closed I dream of you having me pinned
I'm not here
He grunts and forces and thrusts through my plea
His nails bleeding my strength to get up and flee
I'm not here
And the tear of my soul transports me in your arms
Quivering for peace while he takes my last charms
I'm not here
But neither are you now that I've been replaced
Knight swords are my feet, while he enjoys your mistake
I'm not here
I'm not here
I'm not...
Here

ABUSED

Bruise on my neck,
Made by your hands…
A woeful wreck,
From your demands.

Your scratched fingers,
Show your guilt,
My nails, splinters,
From my wilt.

I turn all blue…
But hear you laugh,
I still loved you…
My Epitaph.

TOOTHLESS

Seat at the table,
While I sleep on the street…
Like all the disabled,
That you will never meet…

Take all decisions,
That don't concern you…
The world you envision
Belongs to a few.

The ones who believe
Business comes before all,
And hide up their sleeves
Shame, pity and thrall.

Let us all die
And flourish your green garden,
An eye for an eye…
Await no pardon.

WASTE

No need to fill the void,
With expired affection
As it is from Zeus I descend
And from Olympus, I decoyed.

Athena, my Godmother
Has warned me about men,
Who weaken women with smiles,
And take what they think is deserved.

So, keep your hearts and blown kisses,
And stay where you're appreciated…
Cause my strength knows no mercy,
For those who are time thieves.

JOKER

You judge quite a lot
For someone who went through the same...
I suppose you got caught
In how you play your own game...

SOULLESS

I always thought of myself as having a gentle soul,
But that was before I met you…
Before you ignored my fears…
Before you poured gasoline on my tears…
Before you let your demons feast on my wars while sipping beers…
I always thought of myself as having a gentle soul...
Until you...

STORY OF A REBIRTH

My bleeding heart,
Faltered its soul,
Crumbled apart,
Lost all control.

With a fresh start,
I went to scroll,
Falsely depart…
Sort of loophole.

I dove into art,
Lost my end goal,
Had to abort,
And played the role.

The silence chart,
Was a sinkhole,
So I exhort,
Down the past knoll.

I healed my heart,
Mended my soul,
Became fuck smart…
And killed the trolls.

ARTEMIS

GODDESS OF THE HUNT, THE WILDERNESS, WILD ANIMALS, THE MOON, AND CHASTITY. SHE IS THE PROTECTOR OF BIRTH BUT COULD ALSO INFLICT CHILD BIRTH DEATH WITH HER GOLDEN ARROWS. TWIN SISTER OF APOLLO, SHE IS OFTEN PICTURED WITH BOWS AND ARROWS, ESPECIALLY AFTER SHE AVENGED THEIR MOTHER LETO. KNOWN FOR HAVING NO MERCY, SHE IS THE GODDESS WHO ASKED AGAMEMNON FOR THE SACRIFICE OF HIS DAUGHTER IPHIGENIA BECAUSE HE KILLED A DEER SACRED TO HER.

ARTEMIS COMMANDS RESPECT AND WILL ALWAYS TAKE HER REVENGE ON WHOM HURT ONE OF HER SACRED ANIMAL WITHOUT HER CONSENT.

EPIC

She's a wild huntress,
Made of mountains you can't climb
With the heart of an adulteress
And a love no one can rhyme.

Her body is untouched,
But her mind has been spoiled.
Her silences say so much,
Her voice echoes in nature's void.

The animals protect her,
From the cruelty of men…
But no one hears the verse
Bleeding from her fountain pain,

She's a wild huntress,
Taming her is impossible.
She belongs to fierceness,
And those who become invisible.

SELF-LOVE

I love your scars and saddenned eyes
The pain you breathe hearing their lies,
I adore the smile you give strangers
And esteem that you love, beyond danger.

TRY AGAIN

Smoothie blend of improved thoughts,
Sensing purée of my dead brain,
I quenched on blood drops in a drought,
And I expunge wrong of my pain.

Constant upbeat of your silence,
Wealth of you in darkness glides.
From the truth cliff, I descend,
Sparrowed by what you said and lied.

Matter of life for intuition,
Deadly tattoos of lust lasting…
Regretting limps of secretion,
And past hearsay of forsaking .

Short orgasm of fakeness' likes,
Seducing goats bleating hard wood,
Karmic gypsies or poetesses alike…
Nothing can ever murder my mood

STRENGTH

I stand on the scars of all witches,
On the ashes of their souls and their corpses on bridges,
I stand on my toes to reach further,
Than the stakes on which they burnt when they got
perjured.

I rise on the skulls of all the animals,
Sacrificed for their skins by punitive radicals,
I rise on their furs entangling my toes,
On their guts, ripping their last throes.

I fall on the wings of all shooting stars,
Making my ways to end men's wars,
And bring with me the power of creatures,
That died to save us from a disastrous future.

I die on a field of bloodless flowers,
Bathed in cowards sweat and night scours,
And when my eyes close, I slowly weep,
Having let down the world, from all of its creeps.

VIRGINS

It's by roaring our abuse to the patriarchy
That we will regain our virginity!
Not the one that has to do with our hymen
But the influence we got stripped of as women!
So, rise with me and reclaim your power
Don't be shy, and make their glass sky whimper.

THE TASTE OF MY PAIN

Always be the first to sting when entering a swarm
But don't move while doing so…
Everyone is suspicious of storms,
But no one expects motionless bees, death to forgo.

UNCOVERED

I chased a dream of love esteem
And caught demons of hell reasons.
I trailed your steps made of heart flex
And fell deeper into creeper.
I followed lust, gave you my trust
And quenched your thirst of carnal verse.
I tracked your thoughts, carried your cross
And held your hand with glove's demand.
I pursued you, smiles for tattoos
And tripped on guilt, of your own built.
I still ran fast, hurt and aghast
You ignored me, relentlessly.
I ceased the quest of ghostly rest
And watched you rise with wings of lies.
I let you be, soul unhappy
My game over, goodbye lover.

VARIATION

Bird chirping at sunrise,
Mask falling from disguise,
Rhapsodize.

DEVOTION

Walking through the valley of disenchantment,
I smelled the stench of pride of your contentment.
As you spoke of friendship and pretended to support me,
But burnt in secret for the king of lechery…
I walked into your trap and bruised my ego,
Breaking the silence I used as placebo,
Giving you here and there a piece of my soul,
And emptying my heart for you to gain control.
Old dying flames aren't easy to extinguish,
Nonetheless you were a master at hiding your anguish
Until I came along and saw all your games,
But understood too late you had him in your veins…

SETTLEMENT

I should unleash my hounds,
On those who saw me naked,
Rip their flesh for the wounds
They inflicted when I'm sacred.

Or with my bow and quiver,
Pierce their sinful eyes…
Torch the souls who remember
Every one of my cries.

Or maybe I should kill,
Their taunted progenitures…
A golden arrow for their thrill
And a smile for my torture.

SUNSHINE RHYMES AND OTHER BLISS

" And what if my pain slowly disappears
What if my words aren't full of tears?
Would I lose my muse being too happy
Would I become fake for everyone to see? "

" Your poems don't lie only in your darkness
In fact it can also be found in your cheerfulness.
Rhymes are allowed to be as good as a kiss
When it comes from the heart, poetry is a bliss. "

APHRODITE

GODDESS ASSOCIATED WITH LOVE, BEAUTY, PLEASURE, PASSION AND PROCREATION, APHRODITE IS BORN FROM THE VENGEANCE OF GAIA AND HER SON CRONUS ON URANUS. THE LATER GOT CASTRATED AND HIS SEVERED GENITALIA FELL FROM THE HEAVENS INTO THE SEA. FROM THE FOAM, APHRODITE ROSE, FULLY GROWN FROM THE WAVES' FROTH. BORN A GODDESS, SHE FULLY EMBRACE HER POWER, SPREADING LOVE AND DESIRE (AS WELL AS PUNISHMENT AND HEARTBREAK) AMONGST THE GODS AND HUMANS.

SHE GAVE BIRTH TO EROS, DEIMUS (FEAR), PHOBUS (PANIC), AND HARMONIA (HARMONY), (AS WELL AS OTHER CHILDREN), CREATING THE FEELINGS WE ALL KNOW WHEN OUR HEART IS FULL OR EMPTY.

THE GODDESS

I was patient
I was kind
Treasure of the heart
Ideal of mankind
But I inspired so much more
That I became reasons for wars
I wreaked violence and destruction
Madness, murder and temptation
Twisting values of most men
Their fake bravery devouring their minds
I afflicted them with rejection
Or dashed their pitiful expectations
I fed on betrayal and jealousy
Fed them powers and responsibilities
Asked them to pay an expensive price
Daughters and wives as sacrifice,
I became havoc and violence
Turned into a drug of dependance
And bloodied turned all the white doves
Cause men will slay in the name of love.

FIGHT FOR ME

What is love without a little envy

But a pile of lost babble?

If you don't fight to keep those you love

You have already lost the most wounding battle.

THE EXORCIST

Sparrows, swallows, swans,
Goats, geese and doves,
Hares, dolphins, tortoises,
All answer to the goddess of love.

And in the zoo of my emotions,
The only God I answer to,
Is the one of deconstruction…
To exorcise myself of you

SPECIOUS

Once the mask fell, her face was still a lie,
And so were her stories of love and butterfly...
Even to her husband she pretended loyalty,
Only with her lover was she truly happy...

BRANDED

I search you name
In fields of words
Lost in treasure
Of heart absurd
I search your name
In piles of gold
My darkened screen
Hoping for more
I search your name
In ruins of love
My pride ashore
Your soul altered
I found your name
In fallen stars
And on my skin
Was inked its scars.

PANORAMA

I am a survivor of my own mind,

Sadness might have rendered me blind

But I never lost sight of our love

THE BEAST OF LOVE

I am a ship at war,

A beast no one can kill,

A last thunder in the desert,

A tear of love against your will.

BALE OF HAY

Hiding behind a bale of hay
I feel your hands tracing their way
Up on my thighs, under my skirt
Gasping for more, I grab your shirt.

Your fingers slide inside of me
Wetting their tips, where they should be
I thrust and rub to get more speed
You take my lips, give what I need

Wrapping my legs around your waist
I open wide for you to taste
And when your tongue licks at my core
I grab your hair and beg for more

Once my juice is on your face
Start the last strand of orgasm race
And when your teeth find my apex
I unzip you for what comes next.

TEDIOUS

The mind can't be quiet,
In the jabber of life…
But it sure can start a riot
When I think of your eyes.

UNDERTAKINGS

You made a promise to always protect me,
To become the sparrow of my wildest dream,
But inner desire is never what it seems
And you plunged your talon deep into my skin.

THE LAST HEARTBREAK

You screamed your pain with quietness,

Hiding all your unhappiness,

And while you said I made you smile…

I was fated to be exiled

I burnt my wings on your altar,

Begging for peace, my soul faltered.

I went to hell, died on demand,

Tortured by spells and hearts backhand

As my feathers grew from ashes,

With delusions of certainty…

You lit the latch of my gasket,

With make-believe of eternity.

ULYSSES

Souls never lose their way home
But sometimes the detours are worth a thousand lives.

I just wish the winds would hurry your journey back to me,
but I have learned that nothing can derail destiny.
So, like Penelope I wait.
I wait for you to find your way home.
I wait for you to embrace our fate.
I wait for you to choose me.

But unlike Ulysses' Queen, I shall live a thousand lives
instead of unthreading patiently.
Because death comes too slowly for those who have to wait
an eternity.

ERIS

GODDESS OF STRIFE AND DISCORD. ERIS IS BEST KNOWN FOR HER PART IN STARTING THE TROJAN WAR. AFTER NOT BEING INVITED TO THE WEDDING OF THE HERO PELEUS AND THE SEA GODDESS THETIS, SHE SHOWED UP WITH A GOLDEN APPLE AS A GIFT "FOR THE FAIREST." ATHENA, HERA AND APHRODITE CAME FORWARD.

PARIS, HANDSOME PRINCE OF TROY, WAS CHOSEN TO DECIDE WHO WILL RECEIVE THE APPLE. ATTEMPTING TO BRIBE HIM, HERA OFFERED RULERSHIP. ATHENA OFFERED SUCCESS IN WAR AND APHRODITE OFFERED THE MOST BEAUTIFUL WOMAN IN THE WORLD.

PARIS CHOSE APHRODITE AND THE REST OF THE STORY IS KNOWN AS THE WAR OF TROY.

INTELLIGENCE

If I had an apple to seed discord
Would I use it or leave it to decore?
Would I be weak and start trouble
Or keep my head low and stay humble?

Would I tell someone's husband their wife is a cheat?
That their smiles are tangled to their lying heartbeat?
Or would I wait for karma to work its magic
Not wanting to paint my own life dramatic?

Is my heart strong enough not to go for revenge?
Would betrayal taste better with truth on my syringe?
Would I be satisfied to see tears in their eyes?
Or is the best reprisal to walk away and rise?

The Gods would say to make someone pay
To burn down their life or torture them away…
But I won't be the one rotting from the core
So, I wash all my sins and swallow the discord.

WRATH

Regardless of time,
Wounds cannot heal
Without being emptied
Of what make them putrid.

Regardless of time,
A heart cannot mend
When it knows its soulmate
Still wanders the planet.

Regardless of time,
My soul will be lost
Even if you find me
Before crossing eternity.

Regarding of time,
We aren't meant to be
I belong to the sun
And you to the sea.

MOLESTED

Why didn't you say something?
BECAUSE I HAD NO WORDS.
Why didn't you tell him to stop?
BECAUSE I WAS JUST A YOUNG BIRD.
Why can't you let it go?
BECAUSE I HAVE TO HEAL.
Why do you play the victim?
BECAUSE MY WILL GOT KNEELED.
Why can't you forget?
BECAUSE I NEED TO UNDERSTAND.
Why can't you fight darkness?
BECAUSE I STILL FEEL HIS HANDS.
Why aren't you stronger?
BECAUSE I'M ON THE SANITY FENCE.
Why are you a survivor?
BECAUSE HE STOLE MY INNOCENCE.

BLACK HEART

I used to run from monsters,
But they would always catch me…
So now I hide under the bed
And wait for them to find me.
They like to play with my hair,
And let their fingers touch me
Tell me I'm as pretty as a war,
And that they would, kill for me.
I used to run from monsters,
Or were they running from me?
I charmed them with my power
And now they belong to me.

DEMENTIA

As the trees shake their heads,
And nature sings out of tune...
I find myself on two legs,
Screaming like a raging loon.

ARISING

Walking in the snow,
I feel nothingness
When I think of how
You killed my Goddess.

You called me angel
But clipped my white wings.
Eased my downfall,
Said all the wrong things.

Battling against mental health,
You held me back.
Ripped me off my strength,
Distorted the facts.

I need to let you go,
To get out of my shell.
Carry my own cargo
and finally find myself…

DAMAGED

I was trying to spare you
From the pain I feel
Walking through the meadow
Where I had to kneel.

I wanted to tell you things
I have never said out loud
How I lost my wings
Falling from a storm cloud.

They took my innocence
When I was just a baby
Carrying wounds and consequences
Of their hands on my body.

I begged for mercy
Not to come too close
But they continued hurting me
And stole all my prose.

So that's why I don't talk
And carry all my scars,
Not wanting to unlock
The ire of the stars.

LIFE FORGERY

I'll spread venom,
Betray your trust
Won't keep more
Of your secrets.
They all should know
What is it you do
When your demons
Come play with you.
The pile of lies
You hide under
The fake mistakes
And raw thunder…
That behind smiles
And certain doors
Is all the smoke
Of two-faced wars.
'Cos the souls' swarm
You eat and mark
Sates your hunger
But kills your heart.

STANDSTILL

Darkness settles on my mourning,
My thoughts sinking in painful depth,
As I exhale in the warning
Of another day surviving death.
Holding onto the chirps of birds,
I await the night of my murder
And find refuge in all the words,
Scarring the wounds of my torpor.
Nothing to say, little too late,
Wishing all well and happiness,
I gave up hope and all its fate,
And drift away in ghastliness.

SHOUTING DREAM

The quiet is loud in my clamorous mind,
The screams of my whispers awaken from the chimes,
The wind played silently like a voiceless crime,
Under piles of heartbreak and barrels of wine.
Words and tears flying as high as poetry,
Fatigue piling on bones with no diplomacy,
Under the weight of love, I curl hopelessly,
While birds tell the pain of my astrolatry.
Crushed lungs and hopes taking my breath away,
Soul becoming deaf from all the lies sprayed,
I drift slowly under the racket of my scars,
Not hoping to be saved by the love of my stars.

MISPLACED ANGER

And the day your kingdom falls…
You will realize…
The one you beheaded with silence
Because of your favorites' whispers
Was in fact your queen
Speaking with a sword of truth
To protect you from succubus
Who were sucking on your soul…
You let ear worms butcher her spirit
And you fed her to Hell
Nonetheless she survived
And forgave you…
But tell me King, will you forgive yourself?

NIKE

NIKE WAS A GODDESS WHO PERSONIFIED VICTORY IN
ANY FIELD INCLUDING ART, MUSIC, WAR, AND ATHLETICS.
SHE IS OFTEN REPRESENTED AS WINGED AND HOLDING A
PALM BRANCH, OR OTHER SYMBOL OF VICTORY.

NIKE WAS ONE OF THE FIRST GOD TO OFFER HER
ALLEGIANCE TO ZEUS AND IS ALSO WELL KNOWN TO BE
A COMPANION TO ATHENA AS REPRESENTED ON THE
PARTHENON'S MASSIVE CULT STATUE OF ATHENS.

WARRIOR

Don't think her smile hides her scars...

It is, in fact, her best weapon against her inner wars.

ALIVE

And again, I rise
From the ashes of my mind
Hypnotized
By my thoughts undefined.
But still feeling the knife
That left me dead behind
Stealing the last life
Where love had me blind

EMPOWERING

Erasing the mistakes that scarred my childhood,
Melting the distress, I fell in my bones,
Pulling the memories, I need to silence,
Praying and listening to receive some guidance.
Obliterating the demons who are hurting me,
Wondering how I become the one I was meant to be,
Exploring the doubts that creep in my veins,
Roaring all the hate I don't want the pain.
Ignoring the voices who are holding me back,
Neglecting the fears of being attacked,
Grabbing my fate by its own stubborn horns,
That's how I fight most of my lifelong storms.

FRAUD

If missing one feather made you fall…
Then maybe you were never meant to fly.

DRAGON

Was my fire burning
What was left of your heart
Or was my reckoning
What made you fall apart?

ATYPICAL

And through layers of pain
And under the armor of destiny
I smile to shine my strength
And hide the scars of my vulnerability.

AUTHOR

I travelled through stories
Without escaping my reality
And chased the butterfly
Across word painted skies…

ENOUGH

You don't fight a dragon with fire
So why would you fight assholes with ire?
Be silent in taking back your power,
And smile while mentally flipping them the finger.

MY VICTORY

Behind my tears is my strength,

Soothing the smile of my failures,

And while you laugh at my expense,

My own struggles become prayers.

You shake your flag of treachery,

Thinking it gives you great power,

But it paints you as disdainful,

And taints you as a saviour.

As you gallop on your high horse,

I shield my heart in my armour…

And while my life takes back its course

You still burn hate with raw ardor.

A POTPOURRI OF FREAKS

I bow to the witches
And applaud the goddesses
Listen to the gurus
And cry with my muses
Dance with the amazons
And fly on swans
Sacrifice with the priestesses
And kill with the harpies
Nightmare with the nymphs
And drink with the vamps
Hurt with the Earth
And sing with the North
I live with the creeps
And their potpourri of freaks
I march with an army
And fight patriarchy
But most of all I stand
With all my allies
And powerful, we ascend
In glorious victory.

The only ones to thank are the Goddesses who support me through day and night while I live this human experience. Their strength is incomparable and their love unconditional. Thank you.

Follow me on Instagram (Author.Gabrielle.G) or Facebook (GabrielleG) and TikTok (AuthorgabrielleG) for daily (or almost daily) poetry.

ABOUT GABRIELLE G.

Real - Raw - Authentic.

Because why write if it isn't to bleed.

Gabrielle likes to say that she grew up in France, became an adult in Switzerland, and is maturing in Canada. Where will she grow old? Only time will tell… but what you need to know is that Gabrielle would do anything for a cup of tea, still celebrates her half-birthdays, and feels that everyone has an inner voice that guides our passions.

Gabrielle's style is fiercely raw and driven by pure emotion. Her stories and poetry leave you out of breath, yearning for more, while at the same time wiping away tears.

Visit www.authorgabrielleg.com for more details

Made in the USA
Columbia, SC
01 October 2022

68463977R00079